WEATHER
AFFECTS ME

CHERS...   WEATHER WATCHERS...   WEATHER WATCHERS...   WEATHER WATCHER

MARI SCHUH

Rourke
Educational Media

A Division of
Carson
Dellosa
Education

rourkeeducationalmedia.com

T0020271

BEFORE AND DURING READING ACTIVITIES

Before Reading: *Building Background Knowledge and Vocabulary*

Building background knowledge can help children process new information and build upon what they already know. Before reading a book, it is important to tap into what children already know about the topic. This will help them develop their vocabulary and increase their reading comprehension.

Questions and Activities to Build Background Knowledge:

1. Look at the front cover of the book and read the title. What do you think this book will be about?
2. What do you already know about this topic?
3. Take a book walk and skim the pages. Look at the table of contents, photographs, captions, and bold words. Did these text features give you any information or predictions about what you will read in this book?

Vocabulary: *Vocabulary Is Key to Reading Comprehension*

Use the following directions to prompt a conversation about each word.
- Read the vocabulary words.
- What comes to mind when you see each word?
- What do you think each word means?

Vocabulary Words:
- *Fahrenheit*
- *foggy*
- *humid*
- *reports*

During Reading: *Reading for Meaning and Understanding*

To achieve deep comprehension of a book, children are encouraged to use close reading strategies. During reading, it is important to have children stop and make connections. These connections result in deeper analysis and understanding of a book.

 Close Reading a Text

During reading, have children stop and talk about the following:
- Any confusing parts
- Any unknown words
- Text to text, text to self, text to world connections
- The main idea in each chapter or heading

Encourage children to use context clues to determine the meaning of any unknown words. These strategies will help children learn to analyze the text more thoroughly as they read.

When you are finished reading this book, turn to the last page for an **After Reading Activity**.

TABLE OF CONTENTS

SUNNY DAYS

Look out the window.

How is the weather?

Some days are sunny.

I play outside.

Sunscreen keeps my skin safe.

Wear sunscreen even on cloudy or cool days to keep your skin protected.

Some days are hot and **humid**.

I drink lots of water.

I sit in the shade.

OTHER DAYS

Some days are very cold.

Today's temperature is one degree **Fahrenheit** (-17 degrees Celsius).

It's too cold to play outside.

I play games inside.

Some days are windy.

It is hard to ride a bike in the wind.

I fly a kite instead!

Some days are rainy.

I carry an umbrella.

Two inches (five centimeters) of rain fell today!

Some days are **foggy**.

It is hard to see.

The school bus cannot come to pick me up.

Fog is a cloud that is close to the ground. When you walk through fog, you are walking through a cloud!

CHANGING WEATHER

The weather changes.

I watch weather **reports**.

The temperature will reach 70 degrees Fahrenheit (21 degrees Celsius) today.

I want to go outside.

It is a good day for a picnic!

PHOTO GLOSSARY

 **Fahrenheit** (FAR-uhn-hite): A measurement of temperature that uses a scale on which water boils at 212 degrees and freezes at 32 degrees.

 **foggy** (FAWG-ee): Misty; when the air is full of water vapor.

 **humid** (HYOO-mid): Damp and moist.

 **reports** (ri-PORTZ): Detailed descriptions of events. Weather reports are often on TV and the radio.

ACTIVITY: Fog in a Jar

See how fog can form, making it hard to see. How do foggy days change your plans for the day?

Supplies
glass jar
hot water
small strainer
ice cubes

Directions
1. Fill a glass jar with hot water. Then, pour out almost all the water.
2. Put ice cubes in a strainer. Put the strainer over the jar.
3. Look at the jar. Cold air from the ice cubes will mix with warm air in the jar. Water vapor will form, making fog inside the jar.

ABOUT THE AUTHOR

Mari Schuh is the author of more than 300 nonfiction books for beginning readers, including many books about sports, animals, and stormy weather. She lives in Iowa with her husband and one very feisty house rabbit. You can learn more at her website: www.marischuh.com.

INDEX

AFTER READING ACTIVITY

On a sheet of paper, draw a calendar showing one week. At the end of each day, draw a picture or write something to describe the weather. Then, draw a picture or write something to tell what you did outside. At the end of the week, review your calendar. What kinds of weather did you have? How did the weather affect what you did?

Library of Congress PCN Data

Weather Affects Me / Mari Schuh
(Weather Watchers)
ISBN 978-1-73162-843-5 (hard cover)(alk. paper)
ISBN 978-1-73162-838-1 (soft cover)
ISBN 978-1-73162-850-3 (e-Book)
ISBN 978-1-73163-330-9 (ePub)
Library of Congress Control Number: 2019945511

Rourke Educational Media
Printed in the United States of America,
North Mankato, Minnesota

Edited by: Hailey Scragg
Cover and interior design by: Kathy Walsh
Photo Credits: Cover, background ©RapidEye, Alex Potemkin; Pg 5 ©Zurijeta; Pg 7 ©FatCamera; Pg 9, 22 ©Robert Kneschke; Pg 13 ©Wavebreakmedia; Pg 15 © Sasiistock; Pg 19, 21, 22 ©monkeybusinessimages; Pg 17, 22 ©Yutthana.Rae; Pg 11, 22 ©KristinaKibler